extreme threats

VOLCANOES

extreme threats

VOLCANOES

Don Nardo

MORGAN REYNOLDS PUBLISHING

Greensboro, NC

Designed and produced by OTTN Publishing, Stockton, N.J.

Morgan Reynolds Publishing
620 South Elm Street, Suite 387
Greensboro, NC 27406
www.morganreynolds.com
1-800-535-1504

First printing

1 3 5 7 9 8 6 4 2

Library of Congress Cataloging-in-Publication Data

Nardo, Don, 1947-
  Volcanoes / by Don Nardo. – 1st ed.
      p. cm. – (Extreme threats)
  Includes bibliographical references and index.
  ISBN 978-1-59935-118-6 (alk. paper)
  1. Volcanoes–Juvenile literature. I. Title.
  QE521.3.N37 2009
  551.21–dc22
                                            2009025705

extreme threats

ASTEROIDS AND COMETS   VOLCANOES
     CLIMATE CHANGE   WILDFIRES

TABLE OF CONTENTS

Mount Stromboli in Italy is known for its explosive eruptions, which can shoot cinders and molten rock hundreds of feet in the air.

chapter one

Whole Cities Shattered and Buried

For the residents of Campania, in western Italy, August 24 in the year AD 79 began as a warm, pleasant summer day. Situated about 100 miles (160 km) south of Rome, Campania was a rich agricultural region, blessed with lushly fertile soils and thriving vineyards. Dominating the landscape was the towering peak of Mount Vesuvius, its slopes carpeted with forests, farms, and grape arbors. Like a giant, silent, and friendly sentry, it seemed to stand guard over the scenic Gulf of Cumae (now the Bay of Naples).

But as the residents of the small towns clustered around the bay were about to discover, Vesuvius was far from friendly. It was, in fact, an active volcano. Because it had not erupted in a long time (at least 800 years), people were unaware of the lurking danger.

Mount Vesuvius looms over the city of Caserta in southwestern Italy. Vesuvius is best known for an AD 79 eruption that buried the Roman cities of Pompeii and Herculaneum.

Bombarded by Ash

The first sign of trouble was an enormous cloud of smoke that, at a little past noon, blasted from Vesuvius's summit and rose high into the sky. As it happened, the famous Roman naturalist and scholar Pliny the Elder was then living at Misenum, on the far side of the bay. His nephew, Pliny the Younger, was staying with him. They saw the cloud from a distance of about 18 miles (30 km). The younger man later recalled:

> Its general appearance can best be expressed as being like an umbrella pine, for it rose to a great height on a sort of trunk and then split off into branches, I imagine because it was thrust upwards by the first blast and then left unsupported as the pressure subsided, or else it was borne down by its own weight so that it spread out and gradually dispersed. Sometimes it looked white, sometimes blotched and dirty. . . . My uncle [saw] at once that it was important enough for a closer inspection, and he ordered a boat to be made ready.

As the afternoon wore on, the elder Pliny made his way across the bay toward the eruption. His goal was to reach Stabiae, a small town on the shore south of the mountain. There he had friends who were clearly in danger. But Pliny, who was also a Roman naval officer, was no less worried about the residents of other towns in the area. He knew that 4 miles (6 km) north of Stabiae—and that much closer to Vesuvius—lay Pompeii, with some 20,000 inhabitants. And a few miles northwest of that town, and closer still to the volcano, was Herculaneum. Its 4,000-plus residents, along with the Pompeiians, were already being bombarded by showers of volcanic ash. By early evening, some ceilings in Pompeii had cracked and collapsed under the weight of the ash.

When Pliny reached Stabiae, he found that he and many of the residents were now trapped there. Strong winds and rough seas prevented boats from heading out into the bay. Large numbers of people were grabbing their valuables and fleeing by land. The same thing was happening in Pompeii, where more than half of the town's population had escaped by evening. A few thousand of them, however, chose to stay and wait out the disaster. So did Pliny and his friends in Stabiae.

A photo of Vesuvius erupting, 1872. The volcano has erupted more than twenty-five times in recorded history, and it remains active.

Red-hot, Lethal Surges

This decision proved a deadly mistake. Pliny the Younger described what happened that night:

> On Mount Vesuvius broad sheets of fire and leaping flames blazed at several points, their bright glare emphasized by the darkness of night. . . . The buildings were now shaking with violent shocks, and seemed to be swaying to and fro as if they were torn from their foundations.

As frightening as the fountains of fire, heaving earthquakes, and relentless downpours of ash were, much worse

Many residents of Pompeii were found in the exact position in which they died, because the volcanic ash falling from the sky hardened around their bodies, creating a rocklike substance called tuff. When the bodies decomposed, cavities remained in the tuff; they were discovered when the city was excavated in the eighteenth and nineteenth centuries. To preserve the human forms, plaster or resin is injected into the cavities, then the tuff is chipped away.

was to come. Sometime after midnight, Vesuvius belched forth an immense surge of super-heated gases, ash, and rocks. The lethal cloud of debris raced down the volcano's slope at more than 100 miles per hour. It stripped the hillside clean of all vegetation, then smashed into Herculaneum like a red-hot hurricane. Most of those still in the town were suffocated and scalded to death almost instantly. The rest, struggling to draw each breath, died when a second and even larger surge struck the town an hour later.

Pompeii was spared these first glowing avalanches. However, others soon came rolling down the mountain. The fourth one plowed into the town sometime after 7 A.M. on August 25. By that time, most of the community's ceilings had already collapsed. The onrushing surge knocked down many walls and buried large portions of Pompeii to a depth of more than 10 feet (3 m). Two more giant, scorching-hot surges struck later that morning, adding new layers of debris and erasing the towns from view. The total death toll

As Vesuvius erupted, many residents of Pompeii huddled in basements, where they succumbed to poisonous gases or died when falling ash caused their houses to collapse. This plaster cast shows the final moments of a young girl in Pompeii.

These ancient remains show the horror of Vesuvius's sudden eruption.

for the catastrophe is unknown, but at least 2,000 people died in Pompeii alone.

Two days later, in nearby Stabiae, some survivors found the elder Pliny's body on the beach, where ash and fumes had finally overcome him. He had given his life, partly for science and partly in an effort to save his fellow citizens. "What he had begun in a spirit of inquiry," his nephew later recalled, "he completed as a hero."

Invoking Superhuman Forces

News of the upheaval in Campania rapidly spread far and wide. In Rome the reigning emperor, Titus—known as a compassionate man—was quick to act. The Roman historian Suetonius, who was about ten at the time, later wrote that Titus...

. . . conveyed [concern] not only in a series of comforting edicts [public statements], but by helping the victims to the utmost extent of his purse. He set up a board of [former government officials] to relieve distress in Campania, and devoted the property of those who had died in the eruption and left no heirs to a fund for rebuilding the stricken cities.

Despite the emperor's well-meaning efforts, however, Pompeii and Herculaneum were never rebuilt. Nor were

Pliny's Last Hours

The great Roman scholar Pliny the Elder showed remarkable heroism during the disaster, though he ultimately became one of its victims, as remembered by his nephew:

[My uncle remained] quite cheerful [during the crisis], or at any rate he pretended he was, which was no less courageous, [for he repeatedly] tried to allay the fears of his companions. . . . [In the night of August 24, he] decided to go down to the shore [near Stabiae] and investigate on the spot the possibility of any escape by sea, but he found the waves still too wild and dangerous. A sheet was spread on the ground for him to lie down, and he repeatedly asked for cold water to drink. Then the flames and smell of sulfur . . . drove the others to take flight. [Pliny] suddenly collapsed, I imagine because the dense fumes choked his breathing. . . . When daylight returned on the 26th, two days after the last day he had been seen, his body was found intact and uninjured, still fully clothed and looking more like sleep than death.

they even dug out of their volcanic tombs in any significant way. The exact reasons for this are unclear. But fear based on superstitions, including that the sites of the towns

The World Turned Upside Down

The Roman historian Dio Cassius penned his account of Vesuvius's great eruption several generations after it occurred. Only a few, brief written descriptions of the event, including that of Pliny the Younger, had survived to his time. However, Dio did manage to effectively capture its dramatic, bigger-than-life aspects.

In Campania remarkable and frightful occurrences took place. [People] believed that the whole world was being turned upside down, that the sun was disappearing into the earth and that the earth was being lifted to the sky. . . . Fearful droughts and sudden and violent earthquakes occurred, so that the whole plain round about seethed and the summits leaped into the air. There were frequent rumblings, some of them subterranean, that resembled thunder. . . . The sea also joined in the roar and the sky re-echoed it. Then suddenly a portentous crash was heard, as if the mountains were tumbling in ruins; and first huge stones were hurled aloft, rising as high as the very summits, then came a great quantity of fire and endless smoke, so that the whole atmosphere was obscured and the sun was entirely hidden, as if eclipsed. Thus day was turned into night and light into darkness. . . . While this was going on, an inconceivable quantity of ashes was blown out, which covered both sea and land and filled all the air. . . . It buried two entire cities, Herculaneum and Pompeii.

were somehow cursed, was likely involved. True, Italians and other Europeans had witnessed volcanic eruptions before Vesuvius's mighty outburst in AD 79. But these events were infrequent and poorly documented.

No one knew what caused volcanoes to erupt. The most common explanation held that such events, along with other natural disasters, were caused by the gods or other supernatural forces. When the Roman historian Dio Cassius described the disaster nearly a century and a half later, he invoked some famous myths about giants who had rebelled against the gods:

> Numbers of huge men quite surpassing any human stature—such creatures, in fact, as the Giants are pictured to have been—appeared, now on the mountain [Vesuvius], now in the surrounding country, and again in the cities, wandering over the earth day and night and also flitting through the air. . . . Some thought that the Giants were rising again in revolt (for at this time also many of their forms could be discerned in the smoke and, moreover, a sound as of trumpets was heard).

The thinker and poet Lucretius was another noted Roman writer who attempted to explain why volcanoes erupt. He lived in the century preceding the disaster that buried Pompeii. And like everyone else, he did not realize that Vesuvius was a volcano. So his chief model for volcanic activity was Mount Etna, in eastern Sicily. Lucretius offered two explanations for volcanism. One, based on existing superstitions, suggested that disease and other evils steadily built up in the earth; every now and then, he said, they burst forth in the form of a destructive eruption.

Lucretius also presented a much more scientific explanation. Though not completely accurate, it contains several elements compatible with modern knowledge of volcanoes:

> I will now [explain] by what means that suddenly quickened flame sprouts from the stupendous furnaces of [Mount] Etna. First, then, the whole interior of the mountain is hollow, honeycombed with [caverns]. Next, in all the caves, there is air and wind. . . . When this has been thoroughly heated and [has] heated the surrounding rocks and earth where it comes in contact . . . it wells up and flings itself skyward by the direct route of the gaping throat [crater at the summit]. So it scatters fire and ashes far and wide, rolling dense clouds of murky smoke and discharging boulders of staggering weight.

A modern view of Mount Etna, which rises about 10,900 feet (3,323 m) above the city of Catania in eastern Sicily. In the first century B.C., the Roman poet and philosopher Lucretius wrote that Etna's eruptions were caused by heated wind and air inside the volcano.

Smoke rises from the crater of Mount Vesuvius. This still-active volcano is considered highly dangerous; three million people live near Vesuvius, and a sudden eruption could cause many deaths.

For reasons that are unclear, few people, if any, paid any attention to this valiant, if flawed, attempt to solve the mystery of volcanism. The vast majority of people continued to see these fiery mountains as battlefields of giants, anvils of the gods, gateways to hell, and the like. It was not until the nineteenth and twentieth centuries that people began to understand the workings of one of the greatest threats to life on the planet—erupting volcanoes.

chapter Two

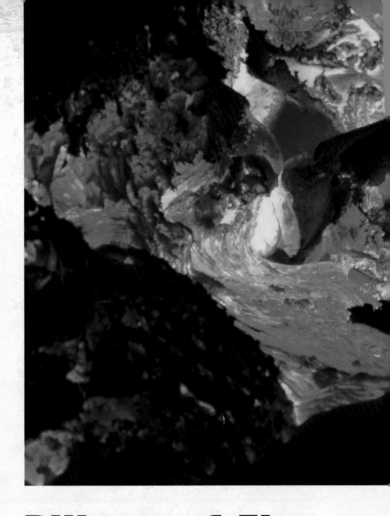

Pillars of Fire and Rivers of Lava

Molten rock, known as lava, flows down the side of a volcano in Hawaii. On average, about 60 of earth's more than 550 active volcanoes erupt each year.

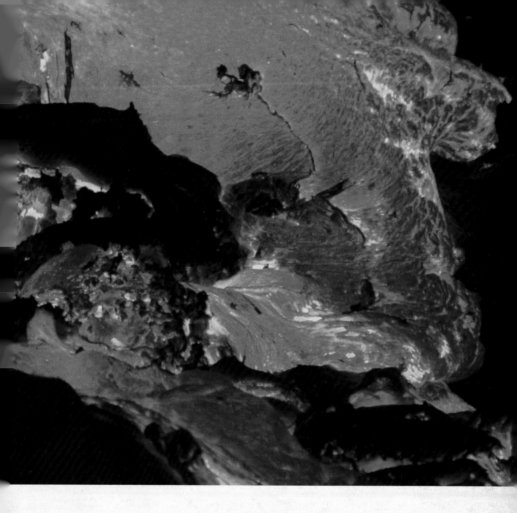

The government of the western Roman Empire fell in the late 400s AD. By that time, the once thriving towns of Pompeii and Herculaneum had become at best a distant memory. And throughout the thousand-year medieval era that followed, they remained buried and forgotten. Then, quite by accident, the remnants of these subterranean ghost towns began to see the light of day once more.

In the late 1590s, an Italian architect named Domenico Fontana was digging a tunnel near the Bay of Naples. His workmen stumbled on some underground ruins that later proved to be sections of Pompeii. Apparently Fontana did not realize these remains were part of an entire city, so he did not pursue any further investigations. It was not until the mid-1700s that formal excavations of Pompeii and Herculaneum began.

As time went on, these undertakings proved extremely valuable to scientists and other scholars in a number of ways. The ash and other debris that buried the cities preserved large sections of them, along with their contents. These included numerous human remains, as well as all manner of the inhabitants' personal belongings. Studying these valuable artifacts has allowed scholars to reconstruct many aspects of life in ancient Rome.

Birth of a New Science

The rediscovery of Pompeii and Herculaneum also raised many questions about Mount Vesuvius and the nature of the eruption that had destroyed the cities. A number of thinkers and scholars were inspired to try to better understand volcanoes and their workings. These were among the major factors in the steady emergence of the modern science of volcanology (a branch of geology). The key early figure in this research was Sir William Hamilton, a British envoy assigned to Naples from 1764 to 1800. Wesleyan University scientist Jelle Zeilinga de Boer explained:

> [Hamilton] witnessed several eruptions of Vesuvius and became fascinated by the mountain. He was an excellent observer and avid student of the volcano, making many trips to the summit, even during eruptions. . . . In addition, Hamilton wrote two books on volcanic phenomena, [which] constituted the first modern writings on volcanology, and, though he was a diplomat [rather than] a scientist, he rightly has been called "the father of volcanology."

As time went on, more and more dedicated researchers devoted their lives to studying volcanoes. They had the advantage of having been born into an age of scientific inquiry. They were not, like their ancient and medieval counterparts, held back by superstition and fear. Instead, early volcanologists realized that volcanoes and volcanic eruptions are natural phenomena

Preservers as Well as Destroyers

Modern studies of the sites of Pompeii and Herculaneum have revealed the stunning destructive power of volcanoes like Mount Vesuvius. At the same time, the excavations show that volcanoes can also be great preservers. Thousands of almost perfectly intact artifacts were found in the ruins. Among them were wall paintings, statues, jewelry, weapons, beds, surgical tools, tableware, and even loaves of bread left behind in ovens when the bakers fled Vesuvius's fury.

Particularly revealing was a find made in Herculaneum in 1980 by Italian excavator Giuseppe Maggi. It consisted of more than 150 complete human skeletons. These people were trying to board boats in hopes of fleeing the eruption when they were overcome by superheated gases. Studies of the remains showed how old these people were when they perished. They also revealed the cavities in their teeth, the kinds of foods they ate, and whether they performed hard or light labor in their jobs (suggesting that some were slaves who consistently performed menial tasks). In addition, the bones contained unusually high levels of lead, likely as a result of long-term use of lead water pipes and cooking vessels.

that follow natural laws and can be explained logically and scientifically.

This enlightened attitude resulted in more systematic (organized) and sophisticated studies of volcanoes. Such studies eventually benefited greatly by the development of new, advanced technologies. Among the useful instru-

A volcanologist uses a movie camera to record the 1912 eruption of Mount Katmai, a volcano in southern Alaska.

ments the researchers came to employ was the seismograph, which records vibrations in the earth, including those produced by moving volcanic materials.

Airfall and Other Deadly Effects

The more that volcanologists investigated volcanoes, the clearer it became that volcanic activity poses a long list of physical threats to life and property. Some of these threats, they learned, are relatively minor. But others can be catastrophic and have killed hundreds of thousands—possibly even millions—of people over the centuries. The realization that this awful death toll would surely continue to rise in the future profoundly disturbed researchers. One of the prime goals of volcanology was to gain a better understanding of volcanoes and their eruptions in order to help save lives.

Ongoing observations of Vesuvius proved extremely valuable and enlightening. Records showed that the great eruption of AD 79 had not been its last. Vesuvius erupted numerous times in later centuries, including outbursts in 1631, 1794, 1822, 1839, 1855, 1872, 1906, 1926, and 1944. The 1631 eruption killed some 4,000 people (possibly surpassing the number of victims of the AD 79 outburst). At least a hundred died in the 1906 incident, and the 1944 eruption destroyed four villages.

Researchers noted that all of these volcanic episodes produced certain similar physical effects. In each case, earthquakes of varying intensity occurred both before and during the eruption. Some of these quakes were minor, but others were strong enough to cause the roofs and walls of houses to crack or collapse. Moreover, Vesuvius's

A volcanic eruption often launches clouds of ash into the air. The falling ash, known as air-fall, blankets the area around a volcano. Airfall can cause serious damage, breaking tree limbs and causing buildings to collapse.

eruptions regularly generated rains of ash, which scientists came to call airfall. The ash often dimmed the sun, impaired the breathing of humans and animals, damaged crops, clogged car engines, and accumulated on roofs, causing some to collapse.

Another typical feature of Vesuvius's eruptions consisted of outpourings of lava, which flowed down the mountain and buried vineyards, houses, and sometimes entire villages. Volcanologists and other scientists discovered that deep beneath the earth's surface temperatures can become hot enough to melt rock. As long as this liquefied rock remains underground, they call it magma. When it pours out of a volcano into the open air, they label it lava. Lava can flow both out of the crater at a volcano's summit or from a vent in the side of a volcano.

Because lava is extremely hot, it can cause plants, trees, and houses to burst into flames. It also can bury crops and houses. In addition, lava sometimes kills people or animals when it comes into contact with standing water, producing explosive outbursts of scalding steam. Lava flows sometimes move fairly slowly, scientists found. When they do, people have enough time to evacuate their neighborhoods or towns. However, some of these scorching streams move more quickly and are more deadly. With Vesuvius's 1631 eruption, for

Vesuvius Springs Back to Life

Many of the typical characteristics of volcanic eruptions were observed in Mount Vesuvius's 1944 eruption. That event was colorfully described by Italian writer Curzio Malaparte:

> [The sky] was scarred by a huge, crimson gash, which tinged the sea blood-red. The horizon was crumbling away, plunged headlong into an abyss of fire. . . . The earth trembled, the houses rocked on their foundations, [and] a dreadful grinding noise filled the air. . . . Vesuvius was screaming in the night, spitting blood and fire [and] a gigantic pillar of fire rose sky-high. Down the slopes of Vesuvius flowed rivers of lava, sweeping toward the villages which lay scattered among the green of the vineyards.

instance, seven hundred of the 4,000 victims were killed by flowing lava.

Cinder Cones and Shield Volcanoes

One thing that scientists noticed about Vesuvius's physical features and eruptions was that they differed substantially from those of a number of other volcanoes in various parts of the world. Vesuvius is almost 4,200 feet (1,300 m) high (and was considerably taller before its AD 79 eruption). In contrast, the most common type of volcano in the world, the cinder cone (or scoria cone), averages only 400 to 1,000 feet (120 to 300 m) in height. Among the better-known cinder cones are Paricutin, in Mexico, and Sunset Crater, in Arizona. In nearby New Mexico, the Caja del Rio region features more than sixty cinder cones.

Cinder cones usually erupt only once. (The major exception is Cerro Negro, in Nicaragua. It has erupted twenty times since it formed in 1850.) A typical cinder

A man observes the Paricutin cinder cone soon after its birth in February 1943. Paricutin began as a fissure, or vent, over a volcanic hot spot in a Mexican cornfield. When it erupted, ash, stone, and lava accumulated around the fissure, building a volcano more than 1,100 feet (336 m) high in just a year. Paricutin continued to erupt until 1952, and the cinder cone reached a height of 1,390 feet (420 m). Volcanologists do not expect Paricutin to erupt again.

Witness to a Volcano's Birth

Paricutin, which is probably the most famous cinder cone in the world, was born in February 1943 in a field located some 200 miles (320 km) west of Mexico City. The farmer who owned the property, Dionisio Pulido, watched the cone emerge and later recalled:

> At 4 p.m., I left my wife to set fire to a pile of branches when I noticed that a crack [in the ground] had opened . . . and I saw that it was a kind of fissure that had a depth of only half a meter [1.6 feet]. I felt a thunder, the trees trembled, [and] it was then I saw how, in the hole, the ground swelled and raised itself 2 or 2.5 meters [6 to 8 feet] high, and a kind of smoke or fine dust—gray, like ashes—began to rise up. . . . Immediately more smoke began to rise with a hiss or whistle, loud and continuous; and there was a smell of sulfur.

Within a week, Paricutin was 50 feet (15 m) tall. And by 1952, when its eruption ended, it had attained a height of about 1,390 feet (420 m).

cone spews out ash and small rocks, collectively called tephra, which pile up to form the tiny volcano's body. Most of these cones appear from secondary vents in the slopes of larger volcanoes.

Another kind of volcano that differs from Vesuvius, scientists found, is the shield volcano. Mountains like Vesuvius usually have tall cones that taper upward at steep angles, while shield volcanoes have much broader bases and rise gradually to more flattened summits. Most shield volcanoes form over hot spots. These are places in the earth's outer layer, the crust, where hot magma rises from deep inside the planet's interior. In a series of eruptions over the course of thousands of years, a large shield volcano forms over the hot spot.

Hot spots do not move. But big sections of the earth's surface, called plates, continually (though very slowly) move as they float over a deeper underground layer, the mantle. (This is part of a large-scale process called plate tectonics.) After a volcano forms over a hot spot, the plate on which the mountain rests gradually carries it away from the hot spot. A new volcano begins to rise from that super-hot fissure.

The most famous example of a string of shield volcanoes created by a single hot spot is the Hawaiian Islands. The Pacific plate slowly moves northwestward. As it does, it carries older volcanic islands away from the hot spot; these volcanoes stop erupting and become extinct. The Hawaiian chain's newest and most active volcanoes, which presently lie directly above the hot spot, are Mauna Loa and Kilauea.

Fortunately for the residents of Hawaii, the threat of erupting shield volcanoes is most often minimal. They rarely explode violently or destroy everything around them, like volcanoes such as Vesuvius frequently do. Instead, shield volcanoes tend to have milder eruptions. Lava pours out in a leisurely manner over the course of months or even years. (Mount Kilauea has been erupting almost continuously since the 1890s.) Also, the lava from these eruptions usually travels quite slowly and in one direction at a time, giving people plenty of time to get away.

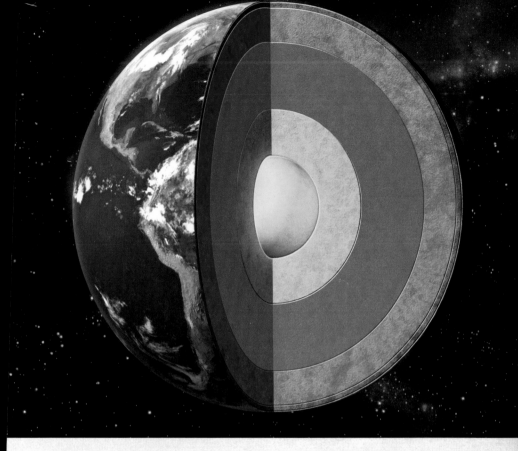

Earth is composed of several layers: the exterior crust; the upper and lower mantles, which together constitute more than 80 percent of the planet's volume; and the outer and inner cores. High pressure in the upper mantle produces extremely hot rock, known as a mantle plume, that rises through the mantle, becoming liquid rock (magma) as it nears the crust. These mantle plumes are believed to be the cause of volcanic centers, known as hot spots.

Formation of Stratovolcanoes

People living in the shadows of volcanoes like Vesuvius are not so fortunate, as history has shown time and again. In the 1800s and 1900s, volcanologists found many examples of this more dangerous type of volcano in all corners of the globe. In addition to Vesuvius, Italy has Mount Etna and Mount Stromboli. Other well-known examples include Mount Fuji in Japan; Mount Agua in

This map shows the location of tectonic plates, large areas of earth's crust that "float" on top of the mantle. Volcanic activity and earthquakes commonly occur along the areas where tectonic plates meet, particularly in areas where an undersea plate moves beneath a continental plate (a process known as subduction). The Pacific coasts of Asia, the Americas, and Antarctica are known as the "Ring of Fire," because the coastal areas are home to hundreds of active volcanoes.

Guatemala; Mount Rainier in the state of Washington; Mount Llaima in Chile; and in the Philippines, Mount Mayon and Mount Pinatubo (which erupted with tremendous violence in June 1991). During recorded

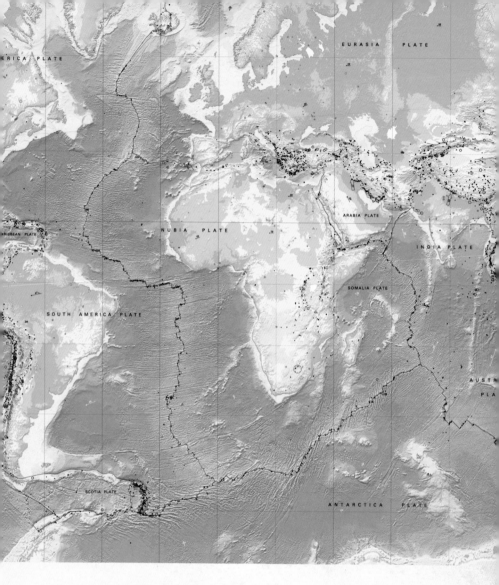

history, eruptions of these volcanoes and others like them have devastated many forests, farms, and cities and killed large numbers of people.

Scientists call these extremely destructive mountains stratovolcanoes. According to the National Museum of Natural History, "stratovolcanoes grow from alternating eruptions of lava and tephra (ash, cinders, and pumice). Both pile up around the vent. Together, they produce a steep cone built of different layers, or strata, thus the name, stratovolcano."

Stratovolcanoes form from the process of plate tectonics but in a different way than shield volcanoes do. In various parts of the globe, some of the huge, ever-moving crustal plates collide with one another. When such a collision takes place, the enormous forces involved cause the edge of one plate to move downward and under the edge of the other. This is known as subduction, and places where this occurs are called subduction zones. The vast amount of heat generated by the subduction process creates a tremendous amount of magma, which, in the words of one scientist . . .

> . . . forms pockets called magma chambers that may have volumes of many cubic kilometers. These chambers expand as more magma rises into them. . . . As long as magma resides in a chamber, [it] becomes lighter, less dense, and richer in gases. [Magma] chambers give rise to volcanoes when increasing pressures force part of the molten mass up through crustal fractures [that] reach the earth's surface.

Immensely Violent Explosions

One reason that stratovolcanoes such as Vesuvius and Pinatubo are so dangerous is that their eruptions often feature immensely violent explosions. These typically occur one after another, sending ash, hot gases, and volcanic debris flying in all directions. Volcanologists call such frightening blasts Plinian eruptions, after Pliny the Elder and his nephew, who witnessed Vesuvius's AD 79 outburst. Plinian eruptions are characterized by gigantic vertical columns of smoke, gases, and debris that can rise as high as 25 miles (40 km) or more into the sky. As the

A geologist from the Hawaiian Volcano Observatory collects a sample of fresh lava, using a rock hammer and water bucket for quenching.

mighty columns spread out, they can deposit layers of ash and other debris over areas of hundreds or even thousands of square miles.

Plinian and other volcanic eruptions vary considerably in their intensity, explosiveness, and destructive power, which is why a special scale to measure, compare, and rank them is used. Devised in 1982 by Chris Newhall, of the U.S. Geological Survey, and Steve Self, of the University of Hawaii, it is called the Volcanic Explosivity Index, or VEI. (The VEI is the volcanic equivalent of the famous Richter scale used to measure the intensity of earthquakes.)

Each number on the VEI represents an eruption ten times more explosive and violent than the preceding number. For example, the 1963 eruption of Mount Surtsey, in Iceland, had a VEI of 3. That made it one hundred times

Mauna Loa is a massive shield volcano on the island of Hawaii. This aerial photograph, taken during its most recent eruption, in 1984, shows lava flowing from the main vent.

more violent than a typical shield volcano eruption with a VEI of 1. Similarly, the famous 1980 eruption of Mount St. Helens, in the state of Washington, had a VEI of 5. So it was one hundred times more violent than the Mount Surtsey eruption and 10,000 times more explosive than a VEI 1 eruption. Mount Vesuvius's 79 eruption and Pinatubo's 1991 outburst both measured 6 on the VEI. That made each of them ten times more powerful than the eruption of Mount St. Helens.

As destructive as these VEI 6 incidents were, they paled in comparison to some earlier stratovolcanic eruptions. Particularly notable was the 1815 outburst of Mount Tambora, on the Indonesian island of Sumbawa. Before the event, Tambora's cone towered to a height of 14,000 feet (4,300 m), making it one of the tallest volcanoes in the world.

Then came what scientists believe was the largest volcanic eruption on earth since humans began keeping records. The mountain's initial explosions could be heard as far away as 1,200 miles (2,000 km), the same distance separating New York City from Omaha, Nebraska. Airfalls dumped ash 800 miles (1,300 km) away from the erupting cone. Tambora's fury was so enormous that it measured 7 on the VEI scale. It was ten times more violent than Vesuvius's most famous

Mount Pinatubo spews ash and gases into the sky over the Philippine island of Luzon, June 1991. This stratovolcano's explosive eruption was one of the most powerful Plinian eruptions of the twentieth century.

eruption, one hundred times greater than Mount St. Helens, and 1 million times more powerful than a typical eruption of a shield volcano. Tambora's detonations released so much energy that they pulverized the upper sections of the cone, reducing it to a height of 9,300 feet (2,850 m). The explosions also annihilated an estimated 71,000 people. In his classic book, *Principles of Geology*, the great British scientist Charles Lyell wrote:

> Out of a population of 12,000 in the [Indonesian] province of Tambora, only 26 individuals survived. Violent whirlwinds carried up men, horses, [and] cattle [into] the air; tore up the largest trees by the roots; and covered the whole sea with floating timber. Great tracts of land were covered by lava [and] the darkness occasioned in the daytime by the ashes [blown into the air] was so profound that nothing equal to it was ever witnessed in the darkest night.

Lyell did not actually witness this great eruption. No trained scientists saw it firsthand. And it was not until several decades later that researchers began to closely study the devastation it had wrought. The more they learned about Tambora and, more generally, the mechanics of volcanoes, the more they realized how destructive the fiery mountains can be. As time went on, such discoveries did more than increase the rapidly growing knowledge base about volcanoes. They also began to open the eyes of many people living in volcanic danger zones across the globe. As never before, they came to understand some of the numerous, gruesome, and frightening ways that volcanoes could kill them. And with good reason, they were afraid.

chapter three

The Horrors of Volcanic Avalanches

Rains of ash from volcanic airfalls and flows of lava from volcanic vents have certainly proven destructive to life and property over the centuries. However, the perils they pose are usually not nearly as dire as those of another common side effect of volcanic eruptions—avalanches. When most people hear the term avalanche, they think about rocks and other debris rolling down a mountainside. Such an event—fittingly called a debris avalanche—is a threat associated with volcanoes.

A debris avalanche can be triggered by the vibrations generated during an eruption. It can also happen when a volcano is dormant or inactive. Piles of rocks and ash that have built up on a volcano's slope or portions of its cone can suddenly give way and cascade downhill, destroying everything in their path.

The remnants of such a disaster are plainly visible around Mount Shasta, a 14,180-foot-tall (4,320 m) strato-volcano in northern California. In the dim past, Shasta's cone was considerably higher. Some authorities believe that over time it grew so big and heavy that its base could no longer support its upper sections. Roughly 300,000 years ago, a large part of the cone collapsed, setting off a truly enormous debris avalanche. Containing as much as 6.5 cubic miles (27 cubic km) of rocks and other materials, it swept outward, reaching a point 28 miles (45 km) from the mountain. Entire forests and all living things within them were obliterated.

No humans perished in the Mount Shasta catastrophe because at that time people had not yet migrated into North America. However, more recent debris avalanches did claim human lives. In 1792, such an avalanche on Mount Unzen, in Japan, killed 9,000 people. A debris avalanche on Mount Bandai, also in Japan, crushed to death some 400 people in 1888.

Deadly Rivers of Liquid Concrete

While debris avalanches are potential killers, they are neither the most common nor the most dangerous kinds of avalanches associated with volcanic activity. One of the two other kinds is a gigantic flow of mud called a lahar. Volcanologist and Open University scholar David Rothery explained:

> When torrential rain falls on loose ash, the water running off the volcano becomes so loaded with ash particles that the flow takes on many of the characteristics of liquid concrete, and is described by the

Indonesian word "lahar.". . . An initially dilute lahar is capable of multiplying its volume several-fold if it incorporates extra material picked up by erosion, particularly when channeled through a narrow valley [such as a riverbed]. Bridges and roads tend to be destroyed in this part of a lahar, but the greatest loss of life usually occurs where a lahar is able to spread out beyond the confines of a valley.

Among the most vivid and terrifying lahars in recent times were those generated by the historic 1980 eruption of Mount St. Helens. That stratovolcano had been dormant for more than a century, so most people were surprised

A lahar, or volcanic mudslide, covers the Colombian town of Armero, 1985. The lahar, which occurred when the nearby Nevado del Ruiz volcano erupted, wiped out the town in just 15 minutes, killing more than 25,000 people.

when it suddenly sprang back to life in March 1980. The shattering climax of the eruption took place on May 18. Some 230 square miles (600 sq. km) of territory were demolished, including many square miles ravaged by powerful lahars. In some places reaching speeds of more than 60 miles per hour, these huge streams of volcanic mud poured down the valleys surrounding the volcano. They destroyed twenty-seven bridges and more than two hundred houses before slowing to a halt and solidifying into rock-hard piles of rubble.

An even more destructive series of lahars were produced by the eruption of Nevado del Ruiz, in Colombia, in 1985. National Geographic Society researcher Donna

Melted snow and ice on the north flank of Mount St. Helens triggered this lahar, which traveled rapidly down the valley of the North Fork of the Toutle River, destroying homes and forests in its path.

O'Meara described these deadly rivers of liquid concrete and their awful death toll:

> The explosive Nevado del Ruiz volcano in the Andes volcanic chain has a history of deadly, heated mud-flows. Glaciers at the summit, 17,680 feet [5,390 m] high, melt from the heat of eruptions, combine with volcanic ash and rocks, and surge downhill as huge, roaring lahars. On November 13, 1985, pumice and ash from Nevado showered Amero, a small town 46 miles [74 km] away. Citizens were urged to stay calm but by 7 p.m. an evacuation was ordered. Suddenly the ash stopped and the evacuation was called off. Then, at 9:08 p.m., the volcano unleashed a violent eruption of lava and tephra, melting the summit ice field, [and thereby] creating hot . . . raging, boulder-laden lahars that rocketed down the slope. Over 25,000 people and 15,000 animals were killed and another 12,500 people were injured or made homeless.

Hotter Than a Blast Furnace

The third and by far most devastating kind of volcanic avalanche has often been called a "glowing avalanche." In May 1902, French scientist Roger Arnoux coined one of the more descriptive terms for this phenomenon. He called it *nuée ardente*, or "glowing cloud." Today, scientists more commonly use the term pyroclastic flow. (The word *pyroclastic* comes from the Greek words *pyro*, meaning "fire," and *klastos*, meaning "broken.")

One of the more destructive forces in nature, a pyroclastic flow is a fluid, moving mixture of hot gases, rocks, ash, and steam. It can reach temperatures of up to 1,830 degrees Fahrenheit (1,000 degrees Celsius), making it hotter than most blast furnaces. Another reason that pyroclastic flows are so dangerous is that they travel fast. Racing down a volcano's slopes, they can reach speeds of 100 to 450 miles per hour. This means that no person or animal can outrun them. A typical pyroclastic flow devastates the territory lying within a few miles of the volcano that produces it. However, some of these flows have been known to move great distances. Evidence shows that one that struck the Koya region of Japan 6,000 years ago traveled an astonishing 37 miles (60 km).

Pyroclastic flows are quite common in the Plinian eruptions generated by stratovolcanoes, and they have killed

A scientist with the U.S. Geological Survey examines blocks of pumice at the edge of a pyroclastic flow from the May 18, 1980, eruption of Mount St. Helens.

large numbers of people over the years. One of the most famous examples of their destructive power occurred during Mount Vesuvius's AD 79 eruption. Geological evidence shows that most of the deaths in Pompeii and Herculaneum were caused by red-hot surges moving at high speeds.

A Wave of Fire

Modern researchers did not know about the nature and power of pyroclastic flows until 1902. In that year people across the world were jolted and horrified by the news of a tragedy of epic proportions in the Caribbean Sea. On the charming island of Martinique, the largest town was St. Pierre, with a population of about 30,000. Frequently called the "Paris of the West Indies," it was, in Zeilinga de Boer's words . . .

> . . . the commercial, educational, and cultural center of Martinique. An attractive city, it boasted a renowned school, a cathedral, a theater, and a military hospital, as well as banks, warehouses, factories, and many rum distilleries. . . . Tiers of sturdy, off-white, red-roofed masonry buildings climbed toward the verdant [fertile] foothills of Mount Pelee, which provided a picturesque backdrop when St. Pierre was approached from the sea.

What ended up marring this pleasant tropical scene was the fact that Mount Pelee, lying a mere 4 miles (6 km) from St. Pierre, was no ordinary mountain. It was a volcano. People had known this for a long time, but it had not undergone a major eruption in a long time. No one realized that it was at that moment one of the most dangerous stratovolcanoes on earth.

Even when it began erupting, Pelee did not appear menacing. In late April 1902, some minor explosions occurred in the crater at its summit, and an airfall deposited small amounts of ash on the town and nearby fields. Later, on May 5, part of the rim of the crater collapsed and a lahar poured downward into a nearby valley. Twenty-three workmen at a rum distillery were killed, which prompted several calls to evacuate St. Pierre. But the local authorities felt that such an extreme measure was unwarranted.

This turned out to be a serious error in judgment. On May 6, much larger explosions were heard from the crater. In the morning of May 8, an eruption later estimated to have a VEI measurement of 4 sent a huge pyroclastic flow

Aftermath of Mount Pelee's eruption in 1902. (Left) Scientists examine the charred ruins of St. Pierre. The city is covered with stone and volcanic material from a deadly pyroclastic flow. (Bottom) Ruins of St. Pierre's cathedral and other buildings, coated with ash. The eruption of Mount Pelée killed more than 30,000 people, making it the worst volcanic disaster of the twentieth century.

hurtling down Pelee's slopes. In only a few minutes, it struck St. Pierre like a super-heated hurricane. Charles Thompson, an officer aboard one of the steamships anchored offshore, witnessed the disaster and later wrote:

> There was a tremendous explosion about 7:45 [a.m.].
> The side of the volcano was ripped out, and there was hurled straight toward us a solid wall of flame. It sounded like thousands of cannons. The wave of fire was [over] us like a lightning flash. . . . I saw it strike the cable steamship *Grappler* [and] capsize her. From end to end she burst into flames and then sank. The [glowing avalanche bore] down on St. Pierre [and] the town vanished before our eyes. The blast [from Mount Pelee] shriveled and set fire to everything it touched. Thousands of casks of rum were stored in St. Pierre, and these were exploded by the terrific heat. . . . Before the volcano burst, the landings of St. Pierre were crowded with people. After the explosion, not one living being was seen on land.

A cloud of smoke and ash marks the progress of a pyroclastic flow down the side of Mount Ngauruhoe, an active stratovolcano in New Zealand.

Thompson was right in assuming that the town's population had been largely wiped out in seconds. What he did not realize at the time was that two people had survived. One, Louis-Auguste Cyparis, had recently been confined in the town jail for a minor offense. Because he was in a dungeon deep underground, much of the searing heat did not reach him. (He did suffer some serious burns, however.) The other survivor was a young shoemaker whose house, on the far edge of town, escaped the full force of the blast.

Several other pyroclastic flows blanketed the slopes of Mount Pelee in the days that followed, and some struck what was left of St. Pierre. But they destroyed trees and buildings only, for there were no people left to kill.

Sources of Glowing Avalanches

The exact manner in which Pelee produced these flows is still somewhat uncertain. Since that fateful event scientists have learned that pyroclastic flows can be generated in several different ways. One is when super-heated gases and debris build up inside the volcanic cone, creating an expanding dome of rock at or near the summit. The dome eventually explodes, sending the materials racing down the slopes.

Another source of pyroclastic flows is a process known as "column collapse." In a Plinian eruption, immense quantities of dust, rocks, and hot gases rise upward, forming the characteristic eruption column. Carried by winds, most of these materials eventually fan out and fall over wide swaths of countryside many miles from the volcano. Sometimes, however, sections of the still hot and dense column suddenly collapse. Compelled by gravity, these materials plummet downward and roll along the ground as pyroclastic flows. Evidence suggests that this was how the terrifying flows that struck Pompeii and Herculaneum were created.

Still another way that pyroclastic flows are generated is by a so-called "directed blast." In such a situation, part of a volcano's cone collapses and the pyroclastic materials

The Lucky Shoemaker

When the pyroclastic flow generated by Mount Pelee struck St. Pierre on May 8, 1902, a shoemaker named Leon Compere-Leandre managed to survive. He later recalled:

> I felt a terrible wind blowing, the earth began to tremble, and the sky suddenly became dark. I turned to go into the house, [but] with great difficulty climbed the three or four steps that separated me from my room, and felt my arms and legs burning, [and] also my body. I dropped upon a table. At this moment four others sought refuge in my room, crying and writhing with pain, although their garments showed no sign of having been touched by flame. [They all died within minutes.] Crazed and almost overcome, I threw myself on a bed, inert and awaiting death. My senses returned to me in perhaps an hour, when I beheld the roof burning. With sufficient strength left, my legs bleeding and covered with burns, I ran to Fonds-Saint-Denis, six kilometers [3.7 miles] from St. Pierre.

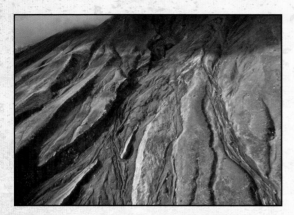

Successive pyroclastic avalanches formed overlapping "rivers" of coarse debris that flowed down the upper flanks of Mount Spurr in Alaska during a 1992 eruption.

shoot out of the mountain's side. This phenomenon was not recognized or understood until the 1980 outburst of Mount St. Helens. After internal pressures had built up for months, the mountain's north side suddenly gave way, unleashing a monstrous VEI 5 explosion. Its sound could be heard 185 miles (300 km) away.

In one expert's words, "The blast was almost beyond comprehension, 500 times greater than the 20-kiloton atomic bomb that fell on Hiroshima [during World War II]." Mount St. Helens's directed blast produced a mammoth landslide and pyroclastic flow that "washed over the foothills and valleys beneath the mountain, [covering] 150 square miles [390 sq. km] [and] leveling all that stood in its way." The pyroclastic flow killed an estimated fifty of the fifty-seven victims of the eruption. Among the dead was geologist David Johnston, who, eager to study the volcano, had set up his camp only 5 miles (8 km) from the mountain's north side.

One reason that relatively few people perished in Mount St. Helens's eruption is that the volcano was located in a fairly remote area. The case of Mount Pinatubo's 1991 explosion, which also produced massive pyroclastic flows, was different. Roughly 370,000 people then lived within 25 miles (40 km) of Pinatubo. Fortunately, at the urgings of volcanologists, a large-scale evacuation took place before the climax of the eruption. This effort is credited with saving many lives. But even then, more than eight hundred people died. Caught on film, the

Narrow Escape from a Volcano's Wrath

Volcanoes are so dangerous and unpredictable that even people who know most about them are sometimes unable to escape their wrath. In the brief period of 1988-94, twelve volcanologists lost their lives while studying these fiery mountains up close. In the 1800s, French volcanologist Daniel Lievre described how he nearly died while examining an erupting Japanese volcano:

I look at the crater. A thick column of white vapors, smoke, and gray ashes is rising into the sky, lit up by red lights that set it ablaze like lightning. At a glance I calculate the extreme point where the rain of projectiles is going to fall. . . . Fleeing is useless. Death is certain. I take out my watch. It is 8:35. In less than a minute it will be all over. I find myself in the middle of a sphere of fire [and] a piece of rock hits me on the head. I sprawl on the ground face down [and] a shower of stones falls on my back. . . . Around me are falling [glowing] blocks [of debris] which make deep holes in the ground and cover me with their fragments. [Yet suddenly] I find myself standing up. I don't know how. Since death has consented to spare me, I shall try to flee.

pyroclastic flows, which melted cars and burned forests to cinders, captured the imaginations of people worldwide. They also horrified them. One writer reminded us of the ancient myths about volcanoes, calling a photo of one of these glowing avalanches "a surrealistic image of hell."

Collapsing Cones and Walls of Water

E arly in the morning of August 27, 1883, an elderly Dutch sailor–unable to sleep–got dressed and went for a walk along the beach at Anjer. That bustling port town was situated along the Sunda Strait, on the western coast of Java in Indonesia. On the far side of the strait loomed another large Indonesian island, Sumatra. In between, in the center of the strait about 40 miles (65 km) from Anjer, rested the small volcanic island of Krakatoa. It was because of that island that the sailor had not been able to sleep.

Krakatoa had been making a racket all night, producing loud, thundering noises. These sounds, along with discharges of smoke and ash, were part of an eruption that had begun several weeks before. Like his fellow residents of Anjer and the inhabitants of other towns lying along the strait, the sailor viewed the distant fiery peak as a nuisance rather than a threat. He hoped the mountain would soon quiet down and allow people to resume their normal, peaceful lives.

None of those lives would ever be the same, however. Looking out into the strait, the sailor suddenly caught sight of something strange and terrifying. He later recalled:

> I noticed a dark black object through the gloom, traveling toward the shore. At first sight it seemed like a low range of hills rising out of the water. But I knew there was nothing of the kind in that part of the Sunda Strait. A second glance—and a very hurried one at that—convinced me that it was a lofty ridge of water many feet high.

What the sailor saw was an enormous wall of water racing toward the shore. For a long time, people called waves of this sort "tidal waves." But scientists rejected this term because such waves are not caused by the tides. Instead, they embraced the term tsunami. It comes from two Japanese words—*tsu*, meaning "harbor," and *nami*, meaning "wave."

Tsunamis were not a new natural phenomenon in 1883. Giant waves had struck many parts of the world numerous times over the centuries. But before Krakatoa's eruption, they had not been associated with volcanic eruptions. For this reason, scientists from around the globe hurried to Indonesia to study Krakatoa and its 1883 eruption, which turned out to be hugely destructive. In the words of one observer, it was the production of massive tsunamis that made Krakatoa . . .

> . . . so very unlike almost all the other of the world's great volcanic disasters. Its scale was phenomenal. The number it killed was unimaginably vast. But it was the way that it killed all those people that still sets Krakatoa apart.

Caldera Formation

Put another way, the giant sea waves that Krakatoa generated were not directly caused by the usual phenomena associated with volcanic eruptions. Krakatoa is a stratovolcano. When it erupted it generated a series of explosive outbursts and a tall eruption column containing ash, rocks, and other debris. Many researchers also believe that the 1883 eruption created a pyroclastic flow that crossed over the waters of the strait and struck a Sumatran village, killing about a thousand people.

None of these eruption effects were capable of generating large-scale tsunamis, however. The volcanic-geologic process that generated those deadly waves was far larger and more violent. Scientists call it caldera formation. A volcanic caldera is a large crater created by the catastrophic collapse of a volcano's cone. During its normal lifetime of tens or hundreds of thousands (or even millions) of years, a stratovolcano undergoes periodic eruptions. Each eruption

Two views of the volcano Pu'u 'O'o, on Hawaii. The top image was taken in 1992. The bottom photo, taken in January 1997, shows how the cone has collapsed in on itself, forming a pit, or caldera, nearly 200 feet wide.

This color lithograph, depicting the early stages of Krakatoa's 1883 eruption, was published in 1888 as part of a Royal Geographic Society report on the event.

produces large amounts of ash, rocks, lava, and other debris. These materials add new layers to the mountain's cone. As a consequence, it grows in both breadth and height—especially height. (In some eruptions, like that of Mount St. Helens in 1980, part of the cone is destroyed. Over time, though, new eruptions can repair such a breach and the cone rises once more.)

It is only natural that the larger the volcano's cone grows, the heavier it becomes. Usually, magma rising from deep underground fills the interior of the volcano. The outward pressure this material exerts is enough to support the increasingly heavy cone. On occasion, however, an eruption is so violent that it generates a series of gigantic explosions, which rapidly empty the magma chambers inside and beneath the volcano. This leaves much or all of the cone unsupported. And within hours, or at most days, it can collapse, leaving behind a big circular depression—a caldera.

Volcanologists believe that it was this process that created scenic Crater Lake in Oregon. The U.S. Geological Survey, which monitors earthquakes, volcanoes, and other natural phenomena, stated:

> From what geologists can interpret of its past, a high volcano—called Mount Mazama—probably similar in appearance to present-day Mount Rainier, was once located at this spot. Following a series of tremendous explosions about 6,600 years ago, the volcano lost its top. Enormous volumes of volcanic ash and dust were expelled and swept down the slopes as ash flows and avalanches. These large-volume explosions rapidly drained the [magma] beneath the mountain and weakened the upper part. The top then collapsed to form a large depression, which later filled with water and is now completely occupied by beautiful Crater Lake.

A cinder cone creates an island in southern Oregon's Crater Lake. The picturesque lake lies inside a caldera, or volcanic basin, created when an ancient volcano called Mount Mazama collapsed thousands of years ago.

When calderas form on land, as in the case of Mount Mazama's collapse, earthquakes and landslides can occur. Eventually, the caldera can fill with water, creating a lake. But when the process occurs on an island in the sea, the newly formed caldera immediately fills with water. The huge amounts of displaced water swiftly rebound, generating tsunamis that move outward in all directions.

Like Colossal Steamrollers

Like Mount Mazama, the volcano that formed the island of Krakatoa erupted repeatedly over the course of thousands of years. Modern estimates date the most recent outbursts to approximately AD 850, 950, 1050, 1150, 1320, 1530, and 1680. During these events, three separate volcanic cones rose on the island, which local peoples named Rakata, Danan, and Perboewatan. In 1809, the Dutch colonial authorities of Indonesia built a penal colony on Krakatoa. It was eventually abandoned, and by the 1880s the island was uninhabited. Sketches from the nineteenth century show the largest of Krakatoa's cones, Rakata, as tall and tapering, similar in shape to the cones of modern stratovolcanoes such as Mount Mayon, in the Philippines, and Mount Llaima, in Chile.

Deadly Tsunami

Among the survivors of Krakatoa's eruption were crewmembers of a Dutch ship, the *Loudon*. In the morning of August 27, 1883, the vessel was anchored near the town of Telok Betong, on the coast of Sumatra about 40 miles (65 km) northeast of Krakatoa. One crewman later remembered:

> Suddenly we saw a gigantic wave of prodigious height advancing toward the seashore with considerable speed. Immediately, the crew managed to set sail in face of the imminent danger. . . . The ship met the wave head on and the *Loudon* was lifted up with a dizzying rapidity and made a formidable leap [into the air]. The wave continued on its journey toward land, and the benumbed crew watched as the sea in a single sweeping motion consumed the town. There, where an instant before had lain the town of Telok Betong, nothing remained but the open sea.

In May 1883, Krakatoa sprang to life once more. Steam and ash rose skyward, and residents of villages on the shores of the Sunda Strait felt the ground shake. This initial activity died down after a couple of weeks, but it started up again in mid-June. Thereafter, the eruption steadily gained in intensity until August 26, when a Plinian-style eruption column rose to an estimated height of 17 miles (27 km).

Then, in the morning of the twenty-seventh, the eruption reached its terrible climax. It produced at least three tremendous explosions, which were audible over distances of thousands of miles. These blasts sent so much magma, ash, and other debris shooting out of the volcano's vents that a great void was created below them. With little left to support them, all three cones cracked and collapsed, creating a caldera at least 4 miles (6 km) across.

The sea instantly poured into the void. Seconds later, several cubic miles of water violently rebounded and

TEMBER 29, 1883.   HARPER'S WEEKLY.   61

THE ISLAND AND VOLCANO OF KRAKATOA, STRAIT OF SUNDA, SUBMERGED DURING THE LATE ERUPTION.—[See Page 614.]

This illustration from an 1883 issue of *Harper's Weekly*, a popular American newsmagazine, shows Krakatoa rising over the flooded Sunda Strait before its devastating eruption.

sped outward in a widening circle. As the waves reached the shallower waters near the strait's coasts, they reared up to heights of 90 feet (27 m) in some places and well over 100 feet (30 m) in others. Like colossal steamrollers, they swept inland, flattening forests and entire towns. Humans and animals were crushed to death or picked up and tossed against buildings or rocks. Many drowned. In less than an hour, more than 36,000 people were snuffed from existence.

Many Ancient Calderas

Krakatoa's 1883 eruption proved to be one of the most striking and destructive caldera formations in modern times. Scientists who studied its effects and remains learned a great deal about both volcanoes and tsunamis. They also searched for and found evidence of other calderas and caldera-forming volcanoes across the world. Besides Oregon's Crater Lake, many dozens were found, including Aniakchak in Alaska, Gedamsa in Ethiopia, Ilopango in El Salvador, Maipo in Chile, and Tweed in Australia.

Examination of geologic evidence showed that most of the calderas that came to light had formed hundreds of thousands or millions of years ago. It was clear that they had had no significant effect on humanity since the invention of agriculture, cities, writing, and other so-called civilized developments. Mount Tambora's 1815 outburst had produced a caldera. But it had occurred on land, so it had not created any large-scale tsunamis. At Lake Taupo, in New Zealand, an eruption in AD 180 had measured in the same enormous explosive range as Tambora—a VEI 7. But this caldera, too, had formed on

This satellite image shows Mount Usu, a volcano that erupted in Japan during April 2000. The volcano is located on the south shore of Lake Toya, which formed within an ancient volcanic caldera. The black streaks over land to the left and bottom of the lake reflect airfall.

land. No people lived in New Zealand at the time, so there were no known human casualties.

Researchers eventually proved that one caldera formation that had occurred in recorded times had exerted profound effects on human civilization and history. The volcano in question was on the small island of Thera, in the Aegean Sea, not far north of the larger island of Crete. Also frequently called by its modern name, Santorini, Thera is crescent-shaped, with a nearly circular central bay several mile across. Scientists determined that this bay is a caldera created in a large eruption roughly 3,600 years ago, during Greece's Bronze Age.

One of the first investigators to realize that the eruption had had enormous effects on human civilization was a young Greek archaeologist named Spyridon Marinatos. In 1939, after excavating some ancient villas near Crete's northern coast, he wrote:

> What really [stimulated] my interest . . . were the curious positions of several huge stone blocks that had been torn from their foundations and strewn around the sea. . . . I found a building near the shore with its basement full of [volcanic debris]. This fact I tentatively ascribed to a huge eruption of Thera, which geologists . . . thought had occurred [in the Bronze Age].

Marinatos reasoned that the oddly displaced stones he had found had been moved by large sea waves generated by Thera's eruption. Geologists and volcanologists confirmed this. They found that Thera's Bronze Age outburst had closely resembled Krakatoa's 1883 eruption with one important exception. The older event had been considerably larger and more destructive.

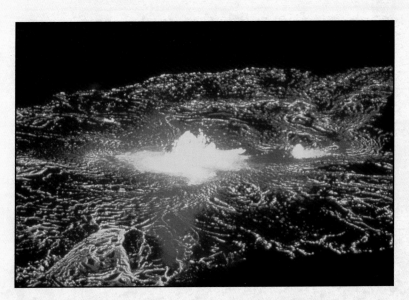

Lava lake formed within the caldera at the top of Mount Kilauea, Hawaii.

Volcanic activity occurs beneath the world's oceans. These vents, called chimneys, are located in the Marianas Trench of the western Pacific Ocean. They are releasing hot bubbles of carbon dioxide.

Burned into Humanity's Memory

Since Marinatos's initial discoveries, a great deal has come to light about Thera's great eruption. Hundreds of volcanologists, archaeologists, and others have studied Thera, Crete, and the historical records of the peoples living in the eastern Mediterranean when the event occurred. They have pieced together a reasonably detailed reconstruction of what happened.

Before the catastrophe, what is now Thera's central bay had been occupied by a massive volcano, possibly with two or even more separate cones. A thriving town existed in the southern part of the island, which today is called Akroteri. Marinatos began excavating it in the 1960s. He learned that its residents were members of, or at least culturally tied to, the Minoan civilization on Crete. Europe's first advanced culture, the Minoans erected many large, multi-storied palace-centers. They also produced magnificent works of art and carried on a thriving trade with Egypt, Palestine, and other neighboring regions.

At some point not long before 1600 B.C., the Theran volcano erupted with unbelievable violence. Its vent or vents spewed out enormous amounts of ash and other debris, some of which Marinatos later found in the Cretan

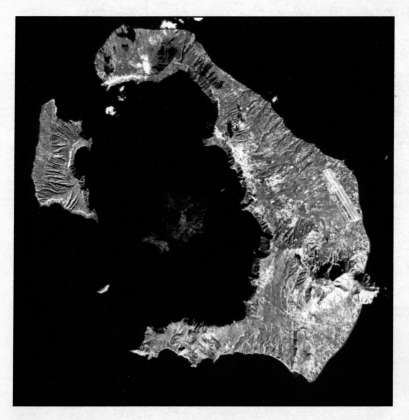

Santorini (Thera) is the large island in this satellite image of the Aegean Sea. A powerful eruption here around 1650 B.C. caused the volcano to collapse, producing a caldera. Ash fell over a large area of the eastern Mediterranean, and significantly disrupted the advanced Minoan civilization on the nearby island of Crete.

A Famous Myth Explained

The original story of Atlantis appeared in *Timaeus* and *Critias*, two of the famous dialogues penned by Plato, the ancient Athenian scholar-philosopher. Supposedly his ancestor, Solon, had visited Egypt. There, priests told Solon that in the dim past the Athenians had heroically defeated an aggressive people who lived on an island in the sea. Eventually that island, which became known as Atlantis, was destroyed when it sank beneath the waves in a single day. The story then passed down through Solon's family, eventually reaching Plato himself. Plato placed the lost island in the Atlantic Ocean; apparently he assumed that it was too large to fit inside the Aegean or Mediterranean.

In the centuries that followed Plato's introduction of the tale, numerous thinkers, writers, and others came to believe that Atlantis was a real place. They variously placed it not only in the Atlantic, but also in South America, the Caribbean Sea, Spain, and even Antarctica. Today, most reputable scholars conclude that the real model for Atlantis existed much closer to Solon's and Plato's homeland. According to this view, the Egyptian priests passed on to Solon a fuzzy, imprecise memory of the Thera eruption, which had occurred a thousand years before his time. The sinking of Atlantis likely was based on the collapse of most of Thera, including much of the town of Akroteri, into the caldera. The story of the Athenians defeating the Atlanteans was based on the conquest of Minoan Crete by the Mycenaeans (the direct ancestors of the Athenians).

villas. After a few weeks or months, a series of deafening detonations, which likely were heard in faraway Egypt and central Europe, emptied the cavernous magma chamber beneath the volcano. Compelled by gravity, the cone or cones then collapsed, creating a caldera some 6 miles (10 km) across. As would happen centuries later at Krakatoa, huge tsunamis formed and sped outward through the deep waters. But the Theran waves were much larger. It has been estimated that Thera's eruption generated at least four times as much energy as Krakatoa's. According to noted archaeologist J. V. Luce:

> The mud-brick upper stories of tall Cretan palaces and mansions could have suffered very severely. [About] 36,000 people perished within twenty four hours on Java and Sumatra, and 290 towns and villages were destroyed. . . . I consider it a safe guess that the loss of life and damage to property were no less [on Crete]. They may well have been many times as great. . . . In addition to the effects of the blast and [tsunamis] . . . the hills and valleys of eastern Crete were covered to a considerable depth of ash fall-out. . . . We can envisage that the Minoans of central and eastern Crete who escaped the waves may well have found much of their land uncultivable, their orchards destroyed. . . . This factor of fall-out could be the explanation for . . . the westward migration [of the Minoan population] which is clear from the archaeological evidence.

Luce and other scholars became convinced that Thera's great eruption caused more than migrations to escape the ash falls. Evidence shows that the event weakened the once powerful Minoans enough to allow outsiders to conquer Crete. The Mycenaeans, ancestors of the classical Greeks, who dwelled on the Greek mainland, took over the Minoans' palaces and lucrative trade routes. Evidence also strongly suggests that memories of the eruption and its aftermath survived the ages in myths. Most famous of all is that of Atlantis. Many historians believe that the enduring story of an inhabited island sinking into the sea during a great disaster is a distorted recollection of Thera's sudden collapse and the subsequent fall of Minoan Crete. In this way, one of nature's most violent and terrifying events lives on, burned forever into humanity's collective memory.

chapter Five

Supervolcanoes and Mass Extinctions

It has been established that large-scale volcanic eruptions like those of Mount Vesuvius, Mount Tambora, Krakatoa, and Thera can devastate large areas surrounding those turbulent mountains. Scientists have also shown that those eruptions had small-scale global effects.

For instance, some of the tsunamis generated by Krakatoa's collapse escaped the Sunda Strait and moved outward into the world's oceans. The farther the waves traveled, the more energy they lost, but they were duly recorded on coastlines far and wide. In Ceylon (now Sri Lanka), water receded from the shore, stranding boats in the mud, then returned in waves measuring up to 6 feet (1.8 m) high. On Africa's eastern coast, more than 3,000 miles (5,000 km) from Krakatoa, the waves were still 4 feet (1.2 m) high. On the coast of France, after a journey of nearly 11,000 miles

(18,000 km), they added several extra inches to the height of the normal tides.

Large-scale volcanic eruptions also cause global atmospheric effects and climate changes. The dust that Krakatoa

When large amounts of sulfurous volcanic dust are released into the atmosphere, they filter the sun's rays and reflect some solar radiation. These particulates produce spectacular red-orange sunsets, but also have a cooling effect on the earth. Some major eruptions have lowered average global temperatures for a year or longer—a phenomenon known as volcanic winter.

A Dream of Gloom and Death

The 1816 "year without a summer," caused by Tambora's eruption the year before, inspired the famous English poet Lord Byron to pen a gloomy but compelling poem entitled "Darkness," excerpted here:

> I had a dream, which was not all a dream.
> The bright sun was extinguish'd, and the stars
> Did wander darkling in the eternal space,
> Rayless, and pathless, and the icy earth
> Swung blind and blackening in the moonless air;
> Morn came and went—and came, and brought no day,
> And men forgot their passions in the dread
> Of this their desolation. . . .
> And War, which for a moment was no more,
> Did glut itself again;—a meal was brought
> With blood, and each sate sullenly apart
> Gorging himself in gloom; no love was left;
> All earth was but one thought—and that was death,
> Immediate and inglorious, and the pang
> Of famine fed upon all entrails.

hurled into the atmosphere dispersed widely and produced spectacular red-orange sunsets worldwide. Considerably more substantial was the so-called "year without a summer" caused by Tambora's 1815 eruption. In 1816, snowstorms and severe frosts struck large parts of North America and Europe in June, July, and August. And in 1817, Europe experienced several local famines resulting from crop damage.

As to how volcanic eruptions like Tambora's can cause such climatic changes, one researcher explained:

Eruptions with high VEIs pour enormous quantities of dust and sulfur dioxide gas into the atmosphere. The dark dust particles absorb sunlight. The sulfurous gas molecules react with atmospheric water vapor to form tiny droplets, or aerosols, of sulfuric acid. The light-colored aerosols reflect sunlight. Thus, such eruptions reduce the amount of heat reaching the earth, and surface temperatures are lowered. Veils of volcanic dust and aerosols can remain in the atmosphere for years. Carried around the world by high-altitude winds, they can have serious long-lasting effects on global weather patterns.

Toba and Volcanic Winter

As striking as Tambora's global effects were, they were downright puny in comparison to those of some much

Lake Toba, on the Indonesian island of Sumatra, is the world's largest volcanic lake. Experts believe that the massive eruption of this volcano about 76,000 years ago—the most powerful volcanic eruption in 25 million years—may have produced a dust cloud that reduced the average global temperature by 5° to 9° Fahrenheit (3° to 5°C) for five or six years.

larger volcanic outbursts that rocked past ages. One of the more recent examples was the eruption of Toba, on Sumatra, about 76,000 years ago. Today, the chief remnant of the event is Lake Toba, measuring about 62 by 19 miles (100 by 30 km). A water-filled caldera, it is the biggest volcanic lake in the world and was created by the largest volcanic eruption on earth in the past 25 million years.

Volcanologists estimate Toba's eruptive power to have been a phenomenal VEI 8. They think that it displaced somewhere between forty and fifty times as many volcanic materials as Tambora did and at least a thousand times as many as Mount St. Helens did in 1980. The dust Toba injected into the atmosphere caused up to six years of volcanic winter. David Rothery described the effects of this frightening scenario:

> At the "worst case" end of the range [of effects], much less than a thousandth of the normal sunlight would reach the ground, which is well below the minimum needed for photosynthesis in plants. This is similar to the situation known as "nuclear winter," which describes the darkening of the atmosphere by stratospheric dust caused by nuclear war. Thus, at its worst, a Toba-scale eruption would arrest plant growth across the globe, and if the darkness persisted long enough it would kill all those plants that survived the sudden cold. . . . With the plants gone, or at least very sick, the animals that depend on them would die too.

In addition, Toba's eruption brought on an ice age that lasted about a thousand years. And it almost certainly caused severe famines among animals and humans. Some scientists believe that this mighty eruption nearly wiped out the developing human race.

An American geologist examines the fault line between two glaciers. Lowered global temperatures due to volcanic winter may have triggered past ice ages, some scientists believe.

Supervolcanoes

Toba was what scientists call a "supervolcano." This term, coined in 2000, was not officially adopted by volcanologists until 2003. In recent years, they have identified several past examples of supervolcanism, and they define a supervolcanic eruption as one that measures VEI 8 and that spews out at least 240 cubic miles (1,000 cubic km) of material. (In comparison, Mount St. Helens's 1980 outburst displaced about .29 cubic miles, or 1.2 cubic km, of material.)

Besides Toba, another fairly recent suerpvolcanic event occurred at Lake Taupo, in New Zealand, about 26,500 years ago. This eruption was many times larger than the VEI 7 catastrophe that struck the same spot in AD 180. Other supervolcanoes that blew up in the last few million years include Whakamaru, also in New Zealand, about 254,000 years ago; Yellowstone, in Wyoming, roughly

Humanity's Near Extinction?

In 1998, anthropologist Stanley H. Ambrose, of the University of Illinois at Urbana, proposed the "Weak Garden of Eden" hypothesis, which suggests that the great Toba eruption nearly made humans extinct. Ambrose stated in part:

> The six year long volcanic winter and 1000-year-long instant ice age that followed Mount Toba's eruption may have decimated modern man's entire population. Genetic evidence suggests that human population size fell to about 10,000 adults between 50 and 100 thousand years ago. The survivors from this global catastrophe would have found refuge in isolated tropical pockets, mainly in equatorial Africa. Populations living in Europe and northern China would have been completely eliminated by the reduction of the summer temperatures by as much as 12 degrees centigrade. Volcanic winter and instant ice age may help resolve the central but unstated paradox of the recent African origin of humankind: if we are all so recently "Out of Africa," why do we not all look more African? [It is] because the volcanic winter and instant Ice Age would have reduced populations levels low enough . . . to produce rapid changes in the surviving populations, causing the peoples of the world to look so different today. In other words, Toba may have caused modern races to differentiate abruptly only 70,000 years ago, rather than gradually over one million years.

640,000 years ago; Kilgore Tuff, in Idaho, some 4.5 million years ago; and La Garita, in Colorado, about 27.8 million years ago.

All of these eruptions had global effects. They included volcanic winters of varying duration that devastated large sections of the planet's landmasses, especially in the northern hemisphere. With each eruption, many forests were surely destroyed and millions of animals died. In some cases entire species may have become extinct. The question that scientists would like to answer definitively is how many supervolcanoes have caused mass extinctions. A mass extinction is a truly enormous upheaval in which very large numbers of species die out simultaneously.

The most famous mass extinction was the one that wiped out the dinosaurs about 65 million years ago. And they were not the only victims, as about 70 percent of all plant and animal species disappeared. Scientists came to call it the "K-T event." (This stands for Cretaceous-Tertiary, a reference to the Cretaceous period, in which dinosaurs thrived, and the Tertiary period that followed their demise. But instead of a *C*, scientists use a *K*, which stands for *Kreidezeit*, the German word for Cretaceous. This is intended to avoid confusion with an earlier geologic period that begins with *C*.)

Many proposed explanations for this disaster have appeared over the years. In the 1980s and 1990s, a majority of scientists came to accept the idea that the chief cause was the impact of a large comet or asteroid striking the earth. A large crater discovered in eastern Mexico in 1991 proved to be the so-called smoking gun that clinched the theory. Dating from 65 million years ago, the same time as

The extinction of the dinosaurs around 65 million years ago may have been caused in part by a series of supervolcanic eruptions that began around that time.

the mass extinction, the crater formed in a blast equal in power to billions of atomic bombs exploding at once. The impact produced an enormous fireball, giant earthquakes, huge tsunamis, and a long volcanic winter that caused the global food chain to break down.

The Deadly Deccan Traps

While it seems certain that the K-T event did occur, wreaking worldwide havoc, some scientists have pointed out that an episode of supervolcanism occurred around the same time. This eruption created the Deccan Traps, a series of vast lava flows covering a large portion of west-central India. The traps are some 6,500 feet (2,000 m) thick and span an area of 190,000 square miles (500,000 sq. km).

The eruption—or, more likely, a series of eruptions spaced closely together—occurred between 65 and 66 million years ago. Scholarly estimates for the length of this eruptive cycle range from 30,000 to 800,000 years. The outbursts seem to have begun shortly before the K-T impact and may have continued for a while afterward. (An alternate theory suggests that a fragment of the comet or asteroid that struck Mexico crashed into India; and the impact was so violent that it tore open the earth's crust and triggered the eruptions. However, those who support this view are outnumbered by those who think the eruptions sprang from an existing hot spot shortly before the K-T impact.)

Whenever the supervolcanic eruptions began, nearly all of the researchers agree that they are likely to have produced many effects similar to those of a large impact event. By itself, the eruptive cycle could have raised average global temperatures by up to 8 degrees Celsius (14 degrees Fahrenheit). That is enough to create a long period of pronounced global warming. Such a sudden climatic change can wipe out many species and put serious stress on many others. French geophysicist Vincent Courtillot pointed out:

Large amounts of [dust and other] material [would] be lofted into the atmosphere. . . . The first effect [of the eruption] would have been darkness resulting from large amounts of dust (volcanic ash) [blasted up] into the atmosphere. The darkness would have halted photosynthesis, causing food chains to collapse. . . . Life would also have been confronted by large-scale toxic acid rain. . . . [One study] estimated that the Deccan Traps injected up to 30 trillion tons of carbon dioxide, six trillion tons of sulfur, and 60 billion tons of halogens (reactive elements such as chlorine and fluorine) into the lower atmosphere over a few hundred years.

The dinosaurs and the other species that met their doom 65 million years ago may have been on the receiving end of a rare double global catastrophe. In fact, it is the only mass extinction known to have been caused by both an extraterrestrial impact and a giant volcanic eruption. As French scientist Ann-Lise Chenet put it, "Our view is that [the K-T] impact added to the stress already generated by an ongoing massive eruption, enhancing significantly the extent of the extinction, which would however have taken place even if the impact had not occurred."

The Permian Extinction

Impressed by the apparent role of supervolcanism in the dinosaurs' demise, scientists searched for evidence of a similar role in other mass extinctions—and they found it. The largest of all these "great dyings," as they are sometimes called, occurred about 251 million years ago. It is variously called the Permian extinction and the Permian-Triassic event. (These terms refer to the simultaneous end of the Permian period and beginning of the Triassic period.) The catastrophe was so huge that it almost wiped the planet clean of life. Roughly 96 percent of all marine species died out, along with more than 70 percent of all land species.

For a long time, scientists could not conceive of a believable cause for such a horrendous disaster. But eventually they offered several explanations, including an asteroid strike similar to the K-T event. To date, however, the most widely accepted theory is an episode of supervolcanism that was even larger than the one that created the Deccan Traps. Supporters point out that the Permian extinction occurred at the same time as the formation of the Siberian Traps (in Siberia, a desolate region of Russia).

It was not simply that the Siberian eruption was enormous and pumped vast amounts of ash and noxious gases into the atmosphere. Some scientists, including British geologist Paul Wignall, believe that the eruption also triggered a secondary calamity. The heat produced by the ongoing volcanism, they say, may have caused a large-scale melting of methane hydrate. A kind of ice, it exists in large quantities on the ocean floors. The release of so

Fossil of a trilobite, a type of marine creature that was once abundant in the world's seas. Trilobites died out in the Permian mass extinction about 250 million years ago, which some scientists believe may have been caused by volcanic activity in Siberia.

much methane would have been catastrophic. That gas is forty-five times more efficient than carbon dioxide (the chief culprit in modern global warming) in raising atmospheric temperatures.

If Wignall and the others are right, "it seems likely there were *two* Permian killers." In the words of one expert observer:

> The Siberian Traps did erupt, contributing first to a nuclear winter cooling effect (caused by dust) and then to global warming (due to greenhouse gases). Over 40,000 years, some land animals gradually died out while life in the seas lived relatively calmly on, as the water temperature gently rose. Then the seas gave up their frozen methane. In just 5,000 years, there was massive loss of species from the world's oceans. In a third and final phase of the extinction, the Permian killer returned to stalk the land for another 35,000 years. By the end of that process, [most] of the Earth's species were extinct.

Such descriptions of ancient worldwide disasters can conjure up frightening images of death and destruction. Even scarier is the prospect of such a shattering event happening today. Unfortunately for humankind, several supervolcanoes in various corners of the globe are still active and dangerous. And three of them are located in the continental United States.

chapter Six

A Grim and Scary Volcanic Future

Fiery lava from Mount Kilauea pours into the
Pacific Ocean, creating clouds of steam.

One of the chief reasons that scientists so avidly study previous volcanic eruptions is that they tell a great deal about future volcanic threats. The grim fact is that our planet is still volcanically active. Some formerly dangerous volcanoes have become extinct, so they will never erupt again. But many others that appear quiet are merely dormant, or resting. They will spring back to life sooner or later. What's more, new volcanoes will appear in places where none existed before. The sudden birth of Paricutin in Mexico only a few decades ago is only one of several examples.

What makes the prospect of future volcanism particularly scary is that human populations and habitations are much larger than in past ages. In medieval times, and even more so in ancient times, human communities were mostly small and spread thinly across the planet's surface. So the chances of any single volcanic eruption killing large numbers of people were small.

Today, the world has more than 6 billion people. And roughly 10 percent—more than 600 million—of them live in volcanic danger zones. Large portions of Japan's and Indonesia's inhabitants live uncomfortably close to active volcanoes. Seattle, a U.S. city with close to 600,000 residents, rests only 54 miles (87 km) from Mount Rainier, one of the more dangerous volcanoes in the world. When that mountain's next outburst will occur remains unknown. But volcanologists say it is only a matter of time.

The flat floor of the Puyallup River valley near Orting, Washington, was formed 500 years ago by a volcanic lahar from Mount Rainier (in background). Today, hundreds of thousands of people live in areas that would be destroyed by lahars if the glacier-covered Mount Rainier were to erupt. Scientists with the U.S. Geological Survey believe that lahars from Mount Rainier would devastate Seattle, Tacoma, and other densely populated areas.

And when that time comes, huge airfalls of ash, scorching-hot pyroclastic flows, and swift-moving, lethal lahars could conceivably kill tens of thousands of people in the region.

Giant Volcanic Landslides

Even bigger volcanic threats lurk in places where the danger is far less obvious than it is from such classic erupting cones as Mount Rainier, Mount St. Helens, and Mount Vesuvius. Scientists began serious studies of one such threat only in recent years. Namely, large-scale landslides triggered by volcanic activity could plunge into the sea and generate huge tsunamis.

The most controversial example studied and debated by scientists so far is Cumbre Vieja. That volcano is located on La Palma, one of the Canary Islands (located off Africa's northwestern coast). After examining the volcano up close, two geologists concluded that its last eruption, in 1949, had weakened its western flank. There is a danger, they said, that a future eruption could cause that entire section of the mountain to slide into the ocean. A giant landslide would displace large amounts of water, which would travel outward as giant tsunamis. These would rapidly cross the Atlantic and strike the densely populated eastern coast of the United States. David Rothery described the potential size, speed, and destructive power of such waves:

> The scale of the tsunami waves generated by a collapse depends on the speed of collapse and the extent to which the collapsing flank of the volcano breaks apart before it hits the ocean. Blocks of 1 km in size would cause bigger waves than a continuous stream of smaller lumps. In this "worst case" scenario for a collapse of Cumbre Vieja, the initial wave would be

over 600 m [1,970 feet] high. It would lose height rapidly as it traveled away from its source, but could mount up again to about 50 m [165 feet] as it broke across the coast of America, where it would surge up to 20 km [12 miles] inland. The tsunami would travel across the ocean at roughly the speed of a jet aircraft, giving only a few hours warning, which is too short for an effective evacuation of a population largely unaware of the possibility of such an event.

Some say that such a frightening scenario is not unprecedented. They point out that another Canary Island volcano, Hierro, partially collapsed into the sea about 120,000 years ago. And evidence found in the Bahamas, situated southeast of Florida, shows that the tsunamis the landslide created were 65 feet (20 m) high when they struck those islands.

These facts aside, even the geologists who sounded the warning about Cumbre Vieja have said that such a disaster is not likely to happen any time soon. One of them, Simon Day, stated:

> It's something we're concerned about, not because we're saying it's imminent. The landslides are triggered by eruptions and are fairly infrequent. And the next eruption isn't necessarily the one that's going to cause the collapse. There may be many more eruptions before the volcano eventually collapses.

Day added that Cumbre Vieja's eruptions occur on average once every two hundred years. So it may be hundreds or thousands of years before the next large landslide takes place. Nevertheless, he hastened to forecast: "It's something that we think is going to be geologically inevitable, because this part of the volcano has collapsed very frequently in the past."

(Top) Satellite photograph showing the Cumbre Vieja volcano, pocked with cinder cones and craters, on Isla de la Palma in the Atlantic Ocean. Scientists fear that a major eruption of Cumbre Vieja might result in a tsunami that would strike North America with devastating force. (Bottom) This photo of Aceh, Sumatra, hit by a tsunami in December 2004, shows the destruction such a giant wave can cause.

Three Volcanic Monsters

A possibly more imminent and even more destructive volcanic threat to the United States comes from some of its most picturesque parks. This menace takes the form of three supervolcanoes, each of which has erupted in the past and will erupt again in the future. One is the Valles Caldera, in northern New Mexico. Its 175-square-mile caldera formed in a major eruption 1.2 million years ago. It has been estimated that the event was some 2,000 times more powerful than Mount St. Helens's 1980 outburst. A second supervolcano lies in wait beneath Long Valley, in east-central California. Its 200-square-mile (500 sq. km) crater formed about 760,000 years ago in an eruption that was 2,000 to 3,000 times bigger than that of Mount St. Helens.

The third and potentially most dangerous of the three volcanic monsters in America is located beneath Yellowstone National Park, in northwestern Wyoming. It erupted three times in recent geologic times—2.1 million years ago, 1.3 million years ago, and 640,000 years ago. The earliest of these outbursts was thousands of times larger than that of Mount St. Helens and created a caldera some 60 miles (100 km) across. Most of the park lies within this and other calderas produced in ancient eruptions.

Like many other supervolcanoes, Yellowstone has no volcanic cone. Instead, the volcano consists of a hot spot similar to the one lying thousands of feet beneath the Hawaiian Islands. Scientists think the Yellowstone hot spot lies about 30 miles (50 km) underground and measures about 300 miles (480 km) wide by more than 350

Yellowstone's geysers (such as Old Faithful, top) and hot springs (bottom) reflect volcanic activity occurring in a hot spot deep beneath the ground.

miles (560) thick. It consists of layers of magma and hot rock. And it generates about thirty times more heat than other similar-sized areas of the American West. This excess heat is largely responsible for Yellowstone's

Volcanoes on Other Worlds

Many people find it fascinating that Earth is not the only planet that experiences volcanic eruptions. (However, it is the only known planet on which living things are threatened by volcanism.) Scientific studies have revealed that several planets and large planetary moons in our own solar system have volcanoes. Evidence shows, for instance, that volcanic eruptions significantly reshaped Venus's surface about 500 million years ago. That planet's biggest volcano, Maat Mons, may still be active.

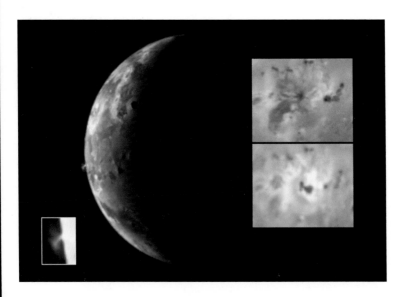

famous hot springs, geysers, mudpots, fumaroles, and other geothermal features. There are more than 10,000 of these features in the park, and each year several million people visit Yellowstone to see them.

(Opposite) This photo taken by NASA's *Galileo* spacecraft in 1996 shows a blue-colored volcanic plume extending about 60 miles (100 km) into space from Jupiter's moon Io. The inset photos on the right show how the area around Io's volcano Ra Patera—an area approximately the size of New Jersey—has changed due to volcanic activity between 1979 (top) and 1996.

Meanwhile, orbiting satellites have revealed several large shield volcanoes on Mars. Scientists call the most massive one Olympus Mons. Towering to 16.7 miles (27 km), three times the height of Earth's tallest peak, Mount Everest, it is the tallest mountain of any kind in the solar system. Olympus Mons's last eruption may have taken place as recently as 2 million years ago.

The most volcanically active body in the solar system is Io, one of Jupiter's four largest moons. Io's Connecticut-size volcano Loki has a 125-mile-wide crater at its summit and emits as much heat as the entire planet Earth. The solar system also features several examples of a highly peculiar kind of volcano. Called a cryovolcano, it spews out water and liquid nitrogen instead of lava. Cryovolcanoes, which can exist only in extremely cold environments, have been identified on Jupiter's moon Europa, Neptune's moon Triton, and Saturn's moon Enceladus.

Millions Could Die

Geologist and science writer Larry O'Hanlon makes the point that, although large supervolcanic events happen infrequently, supervolcanoes like Yellowstone still pose an ever-present danger to humanity:

> There is no argument that a major eruption at Yellowstone in modern times would be devastating. It would obliterate the national park and nearby communities, spread ground-glass-like volcanic ash from the Pacific coast to the Midwest, and cause worldwide weather changes from the airborne dust and gases. . . . A modern full-force Yellowstone eruption could kill millions, directly and indirectly, and would make every volcano in recorded human history look minor by comparison. Fortunately, "super-eruptions" from supervolcanoes have occurred on a geologic time scale so vast that a study by the Geological Society of London declared an eruption on the magnitude of Yellowstone's biggest (the Huckleberry Ridge eruption 2.1 million years ago) occurs somewhere on the planet only about once every million years. But there are several levels of eruptions smaller than Huckleberry Ridge and yet still much larger and more destructive than any volcano ever witnessed by modern man.

"It Could Be Tomorrow"

Eruptions of Yellowstone and other volcanoes like it occur when the volcanic materials in the upper reaches of the hot spot break through to the surface. As respected volcanologist Steve Sparks put it:

What happens at the beginning of a super eruption is that the pressure builds up in the magma chamber and then the roof of the magma chamber cracks. The magma [soon] reaches the earth's surface [and] spontaneously disintegrates and explodes. And that's really why we get such dramatically violent explosive eruptions [from] supervolcanos.

These violent explosions produce outpourings of ash, lava, and pyroclastic flows on a much larger scale than those of conventional Plinian eruptions. Yellowstone's prior outbursts occurred before humans had migrated into North America, so animals were the only victims. But if the volcano were to erupt in the near future, the loss of life and property could well be greater than in any other single disaster in human history. "It's not impossible," volcanologist Bill McGuire remarks, "for a future super eruption at Yellowstone to kill more people across the planet than all previous volcanic eruptions put together."

As in the case of a potential collapse of the Cumbre Vieja volcano, no one can predict when Yellowstone's next giant eruption will occur. Nor is it possible to tell when other existing supervolcanoes will explode and threaten millions of lives. "It could be that the next super eruption is another hundred thousand years from now," says Sparks, "or it could be tomorrow."

Either way, humanity faces a scary volcanic future. And the only way to minimize the death and destruction is to better understand how supervolcanoes work. That could lead to the development of reliable means of predicting eruptions and thus avoiding their more lethal effects. In Rothery's words: "If we intend our civilization to last on this planet, we must find ways to cope with supervolcanoes."

An artist's nightmarish rendering of the aftermath of a super-volcano eruption. Such an event could devastate the planet, claiming millions of lives and even threatening civilization

itself. Scientists believe that another supereruption is inevitable—though it is impossible to predict when it might occur.

c. 251 million B.C.: An enormous volcanic eruption creates the Siberian Traps, possibly causing the Permian mass extinction.

c. 65 million B.C.: A supervolcanic eruption in India contributes to the mass extinction that kills the dinosaurs.

c. 2.1 million B.C.: The giant volcano lurking beneath Yellowstone National Park explodes with extreme violence.

c. 1.2 million B.C.: A huge volcanic outburst creates the Valles Caldera, a large volcanic depression in New Mexico.

c. 300,000 B.C.: The eruption of Mount Shasta, in California, generates an immense debris avalanche.

c. 74,000 B.C.: Toba, a supervolcano in Indonesia, creates a six-year-long volcanic winter.

c. 1620 B.C.: The volcano on the Aegean island of Thera collapses, causing giant sea waves that pound nearby coastlines.

AD 79: Volcanic materials unleashed during the eruption of Mount Vesuvius, in western Italy, bury the Roman town of Pompeii.

c. 180: The Lake Taupo volcano, in New Zealand, erupts, darkening skies over an area of thousands of square miles.

1631: Mount Vesuvius erupts again, killing more than 4,000 people.

1792: More than 9,000 people die in Japan when the volcano Mount Unzen explodes.

1815: Mount Tambora, in Indonesia, erupts violently, darkening skies and killing tens of thousands of people.

1816:   People in Europe and North America experience "the year without a summer," a cold snap caused by Tambora's eruption.

1883:   The volcano on the Indonesian island of Krakatoa collapses, producing giant waves that kill some 36,000 people.

1902:   A surge of red-hot volcanic debris from Mount Pelee, on the Caribbean island of Martinique, destroys the town of St. Pierre.

1943:   A new volcano, Paricutin, suddenly appears in a Mexican farmer's field.

1944:   In another eruption, Mount Vesuvius destroys four Italian villages.

1967:   Greek excavator Spyridon Marinatos begins uncovering a town buried by Thera's 1620 B.C. eruption.

1980:   Mount St. Helens, in the state of Washington, erupts, sending out several large, destructive mudflows.

1982:   Scientists introduce the Volcanic Explosivity Index (VEI), a scale to measure the power of volcanic eruptions.

1985:   A deadly mudflow unleashed by Mount Nevado del Ruiz, in Colombia, kills 25,000 people.

1991:   Mount Pinatubo, in the Philippines, erupts, generating huge glowing avalanches.

1998:   Anthropologist Stanley H. Ambrose proposes that Mount Toba's eruption 76,000 years ago nearly wiped out the human race.

2009:   Mount Redoubt, a highly active stratovolcano in Alaska, springs to life in its first eruption since 1989.

Chapter 1: Whole Cities Shattered and Buried

p. 10: "Its general appearance . . ." Betty Radice, trans. *The Letters of the Younger Pliny* (New York: Penguin, 1969), 166.

p. 12: "On Mount Vesuvius . . ." Ibid., 167-168.

p. 14: "What he had begun . . ." Ibid., 167.

p. 15: "conveyed [concern] . . ." Suetonius, *The Twelve Caesars.* Trans. Robert Graves (New York: Penguin, 1979), 296.

p. 15: "[My uncle remained] quite cheerful . . ." *Letters of the Younger Pliny*, 167-168.

p. 16: "In Campania . . ." Dio Cassius, *Roman History*, vol 8. Trans. Ernest Cary (Cambridge, MA: Harvard University Press, 1978), 305, 307.

p. 17: "Numbers of huge men . . ." Ibid., 305-309.

p. 18: "I will now [explain] . . ." Lucretius, *On the Nature of the Universe.* Trans. Ronald Latham (Baltimore: Penguin, 1962), 238.

Chapter 2: Pillars of Fire and Rivers of Lava

p. 22: "[Hamilton] witnessed several eruptions . . ." Jelle Zeilinga de Boer and Donald T. Sanders, *Volcanoes in Human History* (Princeton, NJ: Princeton University Press, 2002), 95-96.

p. 27: "[The sky] was scarred . . ." Curzio Malaparte, *The Skin* (Boston: Houghton Mifflin, 1952), 257-259.

p. 29: "At 4 p.m., I left my wife . . ." Quoted in "Eruption of Paricutin," http://www.dartmouth.edu/~volcano/Se17p19.html.

p. 33: "Stratovolcanoes grow from . . ." "Volcano Profiles," http://www.mnh.si.edu/earth/text/4_2_1_0.html.

p. 34: "forms pockets called magma chambers . . ." Zeilinga de Boer and Sanders, *Volcanoes in Human History*, 10-11.

p. 37: "Out of a population of 12,000 . . ." Charles Lyell, *Principles of Geology*, vol. 2 (London: John Murray, 1868), 104-105.

Chapter 3: The Horrors of Volcanic Avalanches

p. 40: "When torrential rain falls . . ." David A. Rothery, *Volcanoes, Earthquakes, and Tsunamis* (London: Hodder, 2007), 68, 133.

p. 43: "The explosive Nevado del Ruiz volcano . . ." Donna O'Meara, *Volcano: A Visual Guide* (Buffalo: Firefly, 2008), 31.

p. 45: "the commercial, educational, and cultural center . . ." Zeilinga de Boer and Sanders, *Volcanoes in Human History*, 196.

p. 47: "There was a tremendous explosion . . ." Quoted in Ibid., 205.

p. 49: "I felt a terrible wind blowing . . ." Quoted in Angelo Heilprin, *Mount Pelee and the Tragedy of Martinique* (New York: J. B. Lippincott, 1905), 119-120.

p. 50: "The blast was almost beyond . . ." Staffs of the *Daily News* and the *Journal-American*, *Volcano: The Eruption of Mount St. Helens* (Seattle: Longview, 1980), 26.

p. 51: "I look at the crater . . ." Quoted in Bill McGuire and Christopher Kilburn, *Volcanoes of the World* (London: Kiln House, 1995), 66.

p. 52: "a surrealistic image . . ." Ibid., 28.

Chapter 4: Collapsing Cones and Walls of Water

p. 54: "I noticed a dark black object . . ." Quoted in Simon Winchester, *Krakatoa: The Day the World Exploded* (Waterville, MN: Thorndike Press, 2003), 377-378.

p. 54: "so very unlike . . ." Ibid., 378.

p. 57: "From what geologists can interpret . . ." USGS: "Calderas and Caldera Formation," http://vulcan.wr.usgs.gov/Glossary/Caldera/description_caldera.html.

p. 59: "Suddenly we saw a gigantic wave . . ." Quoted in "Krakatoa: Harbor Wave," http://www.channel4.com/science/microsites/S/science/nature/krakatoa_2.html.

p. 63: "What really [stimulated] my interest . . ." Spyridon Marinatos, "The Volcanic Destruction of Minoan Crete," *Antiquity*, vol. 13, 1939, 429-430.

p. 67: "The mud-brick upper stories . . ." J. V. Luce, *Lost Atlantis: New Light on an Old Legend* (New York: McGraw-Hill, 1970), 83-84.

Chapter 5: Supervolcanoes and Mass Extinctions

p. 71: "I had a dream . . ." George Gordon (Lord) Byron, *The Complete Poetical Works of Byron* (Boston: Houghton-Mifflin, 1905), 189.

p. 72: "Eruptions with high VEIs . . ." Zeilinga de Boer and Sanders, *Volcanoes in Human History*, 18-19.

p. 73: "At the 'worst case' end . . ." Rothery, *Volcanoes, Earthquakes, and Tsunamis*, 156-157.

p. 75: "The six year long volcanic winter . . ." Stanley H. Ambrose, "Late Pleistocene Human Population Bottlenecks, Volcanic Winter, and Differentiation of Modern Humans," *Journal of Human Evolution*, 1998, vol. 34, available at: http://www.bradshawfoundation.com/stanley_ambrose.php.

p. 79: "Large amounts of [dust and other] material . . ." Vincent E. Courtillot, "A Volcanic Eruption," in *Scientific American Book of Dinosaurs* (New York: St. Martin's Press, 2000), 364.

p. 79: "Our view is that [the K-T] impact . . ." Quoted in "India's Smoking Gun: Dino-Killing Eruptions," *Science Daily*, August 10, 2005, available at: http://www.sciencedaily.com/releases/2005/08/050810130729.htm.

p. 81: "It seems likely there were two . . ." BBC, "The Day The Earth Nearly Died," http://www.bbc.co.uk/science/horizon/2002/dayearthdied.shtml.

Chapter 6: A Grim and Scary Volcanic Future

p. 85: "The scale of the tsunami waves . . ." Rothery, *Volcanoes, Earthquakes, and Tsunamis*, 131.

p. 86: "It's something we're concerned about . . ." UPI, "Tsunami Prediction Questioned," http://joegrossman.net/TsunamiPredictionQuestioned.htm.

p. 92: "There is no argument . . ." Larry O'Hanlon, "Supervolcano: A True Hot Spot," http://dsc.discovery.com/convergence/supervolcano/under/under_02.html.

p. 93: "What happens at the beginning . . ." Quoted in
  "Supervolcano: The Truth About Yellowstone,"
  http://www.abc.net.au/catalyst/stories/s1350403.htm.

p. 93: "It's not impossible . . ." Ibid.

p. 93: "It could be that the next super eruption . . ." Quoted in
  "Supervolcano: The Truth About Yellowstone."

p. 93: "If we intend our civilization to last . . ." Rothery, *Volcanoes,
  Earthquakes, and Tsunamis*, 160.

airfall: Showers of ash and tephra created by a volcanic eruption.

caldera: A large crater or depression that forms during a volcanic eruption.

cinder cone (or scoria cone): A pile of volcanic materials that rises above a secondary volcanic vent.

column collapse: The sudden downward movement of the materials comprising a volcanic eruption column.

crust: The earth's outermost layer.

debris avalanche: A landslide of rocks from a volcano.

directed blast: An explosion of volcanic materials from a volcano's flank, or side.

dormant: A term used to describe a volcano that is still active but not erupting.

eruption column: An upward-moving cloud of ash, gases, and other debris from a volcanic vent.

extinct: A term used to describe a volcano that will never erupt again.

extraterrestrial: Originating or occurring beyond earth.

geothermal features: Geysers and other phenomena created by heat generated underground.

hot spot: A place in the earth's crust where large amounts of magma well up and generate volcanic eruptions.

lahar: A volcanic mudflow.

lava: Magma that exits a volcano and flows onto the earth's surface.

magma: Melted rock that flows underground.

mantle: The thick, mainly solid layer lying between earth's outer crust and inner core.

plate tectonics: The process in which large, continent-sized plates move slowly across earth's surface, often creating volcanic activity.

Plinian eruption: An eruption of a stratovolcano featuring large explosions and a vertical eruption column.

pyroclastic flow: A large, fast-moving mass of superheated volcanic materials.

shield volcano: A massive, gently-sloping volcano built up by numerous small-scale eruptions.

solar system: The sun and all the planets, moons, and other objects orbiting it.

species: An individual kind of plant or animal.

stratovolcano: A volcano that has a tall, tapering cone and experiences large-scale, explosive eruptions.

subduction: The process in which one tectonic plate moves downward and under another, generating large amounts of heat.

supervolcano: A volcano that erupts with hundreds or thousands of times the energy and power of a conventional volcanic outburst.

tephra: A mixture of volcanic ash, cinders, and rocks.

tsunami: A giant sea wave.

Volcanic Explosivity Index (VEI): A scale devised in 1982 to measure the relative power of volcanic eruptions.

volcanic winter: An onset of darkness and cool temperatures as a result of volcanic ash blocking sunlight.

volcanology: The scientific study of volcanoes.

Beard, Mary. *The Fires of Vesuvius: Pompeii Lost and Found.* Cambridge, MA: Belknap Press, 2008.

Frances, Peter and Clive Oppenheimer. *Volcanoes.* New York: Oxford University Press, 2003.

Gates, Alexander E. and David Ritchie. *Encyclopedia of Earthquakes and Volcanoes.* New York: Checkmark, 2007.

Kusky, Timothy. *Volcanoes: Eruptions and Other Volcanic Hazards.* New York: Facts on File, 2008.

Marti, Joan and Gerald G. J. Ernst. *Volcanoes and the Environment.* New York: Cambridge University Press, 2008.

Prager, Ellen J. *Furious Earth: The Science and Nature of Earthquakes, Volcanoes, and Tsunamis.* New York: McGraw-Hill, 2000.

Rothery, David A. *Volcanoes, Earthquakes, and Tsunamis.* London: Hodder, 2007.

Sigurdsson, Haraldur. *Melting the Earth: The History of Ideas on Volcanic Eruptions.* New York: University of Oxford Press, 1999.

Sutherland, Lin. *The Volcanic Earth.* Sidney: UNSW Press, 1995.

Winchester, Simon. *Krakatoa: The Day the World Exploded.* Waterville, MN: Thorndike Press, 2003.

Zeilinga de Boer, Jelle and Donald T. Sanders. *Volcanoes in Human History.* Princeton, NJ: Princeton University Press, 2002.

Bibliography

What's Inside a Volcano?

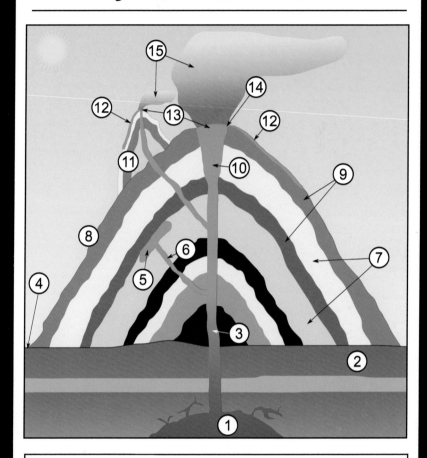

KEY

1. Magma chamber
2. Bedrock
3. Conduit (pipe)
4. Base
5. Sill
6. Branch pipe
7. Layers of ash emitted by the volcano
8. Flank
9. Layers of lava emitted by the volcano
10. Throat
11. Parasitic cone
12. Lava flow
13. Vent
14. Crater
15. Ash cloud

Tavurvur, an active stratovolcano near Rabaul in Papua, New Guinea.

How Volcanoes Work

http://science.howstuffworks.com/volcano.htm/printable

Kilauea Volcano, Hawaii

http://hvo.wr.usgs.gov/kilauea/

Mount St. Helens, Washington

http://vulcan.wr.usgs.gov/Volcanoes/MSH/
framework.html

National Geographic Volcanoes Video

http://video.nationalgeographic.com/video/player/
environment/environment-natural-disasters/volcanoes/
volcano-eruptions.html

The Thera Eruption

http://www.absoluteastronomy.com/topics/
Thera_eruption

Volcano Watch

http://www.ssec.wisc.edu/data/volcano.html

Numbers in **bold italics** refer to captions.

Picture Credits